Mom AND Me

our special activity book

A Mother & Son guided journal

by Erika Rossi

- Ô LINDA VIDA -

SPECIAL NOTE

Dear customers,

Thank you for your trust.

I'm an independent publisher.

If you like this journal, feel free to follow my

work on my website : www.olindavida.com

so you don't miss any update.

I hope you will enjoy this journal as much as I

enjoyed designing it !

Erika Rossi

- Ô LiNDA ViDA -

In order not to miss any of my next publications,
I suggest you to scan this QR code and click on
"+ Follow" on my author page :

Thank you very much in advance !

INTRODUCTION

WHY THIS JOURNAL ?

At a time when Technology is everywhere and children are using it from a very young age, parents can quickly feel overwhelmed. Parents and children are encasing themselves in their own bubble. How can parents create bonds between their beloved sons or daughters, far from the screens?

It was with this goal in mind that I have created this journal: through a shared special space, it will facilitate communication between mother and son, help them express their emotions, learn more about each other, and share special moments... all while having fun together!

You will find questions in this journal about various subjects, designed especially for you and your child. Some questions will be very easy going, and others will be deeper and more personal. You will also find games and activities to reinforce your complicity.

HOW TO USE THE JOURNAL?

Follow the Panda family!

The character(s) at the top of the page will tell you who needs to fill in the information.

<u>When you see...</u>

It is your turn to answer   It is your son's turn to answer   You answer together

There is no order or obligation.

Complete this journal in the order that suits you. Today you're not in the mood to talk about your childhood? No problem! Skip to a section that you will enjoy. Mark the page that you have completed so your son can find it, and vice-versa. If some sections of the journal don't inspire you at all, you can also choose to adapt them, or cover them with photos or drawings! You can write as much or as little as you want.

How often do you need to fill it in?

Some parts will have to be done with your son, while others can be completed by one of you at a time.

Together, choose the time of day for filling in your journal, and decide how often: punctually (during holidays, just when you fancy it, etc.) or regularly: every day (perhaps a bedtime ritual), every three days, or at the weekend if you need more time. It is important that both of you enjoy your time while filling in the journal!

Communication & authenticity

It is possible that you will discover unexpected things about your child regarding subjects you don't usually talk about. Encourage your son to explain and examine his thoughts, to express his feelings, or to add details to his creations. He will gain confidence and will develop his imagination as you go.

Show your son that perfection doesn't exist, and that it is completely okay to not be perfect. Don't stress about always finding the perfect sentences or making mistakes (by crossing out words for example) and encourage him to write something down even when he is stuck on a subject, and even if it is incomplete.

Writing is a great way to exteriorize and detangle your thoughts. It is time to discuss what you never had the chance to say. Be honest in your writings: say clearly what you know and what you don't know and encourage your child to do the same. Show them that they can open up without worries by defining rules: for example, "What is written in this journal will stay between us," or "We will not judge the other person's answer."

Stay tuned and try to understand what your son is trying to tell you. On certain occasions, maybe he needs you to intervene and do some things for him, while other times he simply needs you to lend an ear while he deals with things all by himself.

Have fun!

Colorize, draw, cut and glue magazine images, photos, circle, underline with lots of colors, add bubbles and make your characters speak... This journal is only for the two of you: personalize it as much as you want!

Date your journal and read it again in a few years to make the enjoyment last and to remind yourself of how much you love each other... This journal is only the beginning of a new adventure and a dynamic change for a future to enjoy together!

Grab your pens...! ;)

Erika Rossi
– Ô LINDA VIDA –

YOU & ME

TOGETHER

Our first names and last names :

_____

_____

We are calling each other with these nicknames :

_____

_____

We are _____ and _____ years old.

TODAY WE ARE STARTING OUR JOURNAL :

_____

OUR JOURNAL GUIDELINES

TOGETHER

WE DECIDE HOW WE USE OUR JOURNAL

1 By completing this journal, we would like :

- [ ] To create new memories
- [ ] To learn to know each other better
- [ ] Have great times together
- [ ] Have fun
- [ ] Become professional writers
- [ ] _____

2 Does this journal need to stay secret ?

- [ ] Top secret, nobody else can read it.
- [ ] Everybody can read it.
- [ ] Only these people can read it :

_____

3 When do we write in our journal and how long do we have to complete it and give it back to the other?

_____

_____

_____

_____

4 Diary to be completed by :
   (or no deadline) _____

5 Do we have to answer prompts in numerical order?

☐ yes   ☐ no

6 What do we do if we need more space to write?

_____

_____

_____

7 Do we discuss what we wrote in the diary afterwards?

_____

_____

_____

_____

8 How do we pass our journal back and forth?

_____

_____

_____

9 How do we know which page has to be completed?

_____

_____

_____

CHINESE PORTRAIT

- DRAW, GLUE A PHOTO OR DESCRIBE -

SON, WHO WOULD YOU BE IF YOU WERE...

... a place?

... a cartoon?

... a celebrity ?

... a super-hero ?

... an animal ?

... a video game?

9

CHINESE PORTRAIT

MOM

MOM, WHO WOULD YOU BE IF YOU WERE...

... a place?

... a cartoon?

... a celebrity ?

... a super-hero ?

... an animal ?

... a video game?

DREAM GARDEN

TOGETHER

LET YOUR IMAGINATION GO WILD AND CREATE YOUR IDEAL **GARDEN**

Mom :

Son :

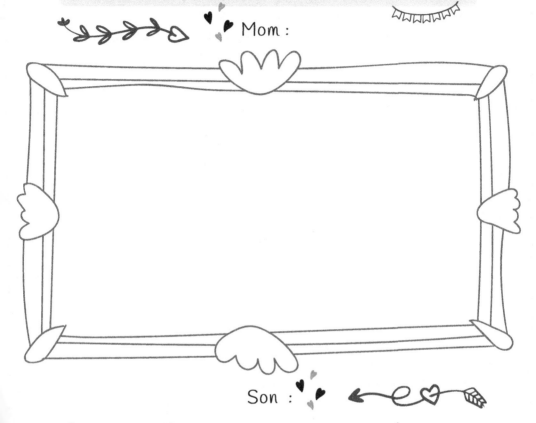

A LITTLE TALK

 WHAT WE SAY ....

 Mom, the first thing you tell me in the **MORNING**:

_____

 Mom, the last thing you tell me in the **EVENING**:

_____

Mom, I wish you woud tell me more **OFTEN** :

 _____

love

Son, the first thing you tell me in the **MORNING**:

 _____

Son, the last thing you tell me in the **EVENING**:

 _____

Son, I wish you woud tell me more **OFTEN** :

_____

SUPER QUIZ

SON, HOW WELL DO YOU KNOW YOUR MOM?

MOM CONFIRMS
(OR NOT)

1) What are my favorite activities?

TRUE FALSE
☐ ☐

2) What do I like?

TRUE FALSE
☐ ☐

3) What do I dislike ?

TRUE FALSE
☐ ☐

4) What do I do when you're not here?

TRUE FALSE
☐ ☐

5) What do I like to eat?

TRUE FALSE
☐ ☐

6) What am I good at ?

TRUE FALSE
☐ ☐

7) What can't I do ?

TRUE FALSE
☐ ☐

(COUNT HOW MANY RIGHT ANSWERS)

Son, you have _____ right answers!

SUPER QUIZ

MOM, HOW WELL DO YOU KNOW YOUR SON?

SON CONFIRMS
(OR NOT)

1) What are my favorite activities?

_____ TRUE FALSE

☐ ☐

_____

2) What do I like?

_____ TRUE FALSE

☐ ☐

3) What do I dislike ?

_____ TRUE FALSE

☐ ☐

4) What do I do when you're not here?

_____ TRUE FALSE

☐ ☐

5) What do I like to eat?

_____ TRUE FALSE

☐ ☐

6) What am I good at ?

_____ TRUE FALSE

☐ ☐

7) What can't I do ?

_____ TRUE FALSE

☐ ☐

(COUNT HOW MANY RIGHT ANSWERS)

Mom, you have _____ right answers!

EVERYTHING THAT WE PREFER

TOGETHER

 LET'S COMPARE OUR PREFERENCES!

What is our favorite pet?

MOM _____   SON _____

What is our favorite wild animal?

MOM _____   SON _____

What are our favorite holidays?

MOM _____   SON _____

What is our favorite color?

MOM _____   SON _____

What is our favorite TV show?

MOM _____   SON _____

What is our favorite season?

MOM _____   SON _____

What is our favorite day of the week?

MOM _____   SON _____

What is our favorite time of the day?

MOM _____   SON _____

What is our favorite singer?

MOM _____   SON _____

 ## PART 2

What is our favorite smell?

MOM _____ SON _____

What is our favorite type of clothing?

MOM _____ SON _____

What are our favorite store?

MOM _____ SON _____

What is our favorite restaurant?

MOM _____ SON _____

What is our favorite sport?

MOM _____ SON _____

What is our favorite dish?

MOM _____ SON _____

What is our favorite vegetable?

MOM _____ SON _____

What is our favorite fruit?

MOM _____ SON _____

What is our favorite dessert?

MOM _____ SON _____

THE 5 GIFTS GAME

MOM

MOM, iF A FAiRY WERE TO GiVE ME ONE OF THESE 5 GiFTS, WHICH ONE DO YOU THiNK I WOULD CHOOSE FiRST?

Put them in the order I would choose them (according to you).

When we have both written down our prediction about the other person's order, I will give you my real choice.

	MOM'S PREDICTION:	MY SON GIVES HiS ANSWER:
Extraordinary beauty	☐	☐
Great wealth	☐	☐
Super popularity	☐	☐
Exceptional talent for sport	☐	☐
Extreme intelligence	☐	☐

Son, can you explain why you would have picked the gifts in that order?

_____

_____

_____

_____

Is there a gift you would add? _____

_____

THE 5 GIFTS GAME

SON

SON, IF A FAIRY WERE TO GIVE ME ONE OF THOSE 5 GIFTS,
WHICH ONE DO YOU THINK I WOULD CHOOSE FIRST?

Put them in the order I would choose them
(according to you).

When we have both written down our prediction
about the other person's order, I will give you my
real choice.

	SON'S PREDICTION:	MOM GIVES HER ANSWER:
Extraordinary beauty	☐	☐
Great wealth	☐	☐
Super popularity	☐	☐
Exceptional talent for sport	☐	☐
Extreme intelligence	☐	☐

Mom, can you explain why you would have picked the gifts
in that order?

_____

_____

_____

_____

Is there a gift you would add? _____

18

BABY'S MEMORIES...

MOM, TELL ME YOUR MEMORIES WITH ME AS A BABY

What did you think and feel when I was born?

_____

_____

_____

_____

What was I like as a baby?

_____

_____

_____

_____

What's your favorite memory with me when I was little?

_____

_____

_____

_____

BABY'S MEMORIES...

TELL ME ABOUT YOUR EARLY CHILDHOOD MEMORIES

SON

What are the oldest memories you have?

_____

_____

_____

What is your favorite memory with me?

_____

_____

_____

_____

Draw it. ♥

IN A FEW WORDS

TOGETHER

WE DESCRIBE EACH OTHER TO A **STRANGER** ...

Son, describe me in 5 words:

1.
2.
3.
4.
5.

Mom, describe me in 5 words:

1.
2.
3.
4.
5.

OUR 4 PAWS COMPANIONS

AND OTHERS...

WHAT IS YOUR RELATIONSHIP WITH ANIMALS?

Did you have pets as a child? If so, what kind? If you didn't have any, would you have liked to have one?

_____

_____

_____

_____

What are your best memories with animals? Do you have some stories to tell me?

_____

_____

_____

_____

_____

_____

_____

OUR 4 PAWS COMPANIONS

AND OTHERS...

WHAT IS YOUR RELATIONSHIP WITH ANIMALS?

SON

If you have pets, what do you like best about them? If you don't have any, which pet would you like to have ?

_____

_____

_____

What is your favorite memory with a pet (or with animals in general)?

_____

_____

_____

_____

Draw your memory

or paste a photo

NOT EASY TO BE A CHILD...

According to you, what is the best thing about being a child?

_____

_____

_____

What is the hardest thing about being a child ?

_____

_____

_____

In your opinion, what is the best thing about being a boy?

_____

_____

_____

What is the hardest thing about being a boy?

_____

_____

_____

...WHAT ABOUT BEING AN ADULT ?

GIRL POWER

MOM, TELL ME WHAT YOU THINK

In your opinion, what's the best thing about being an adult?

_____

_____

_____

What is the hardest thing about being an adult ?

_____

_____

_____

According to you, what's the best about being a woman?

_____

_____

_____

What is the hardest thing about being a woman?

_____

_____

_____

TOGETHER

LET'S NAME/DRAW...

The 3 most important things for us :

Mom's side :

Son's side :

1.

1.

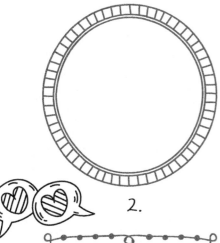

2.

2.

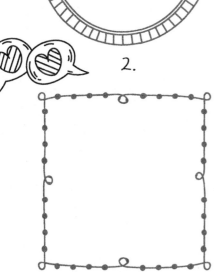
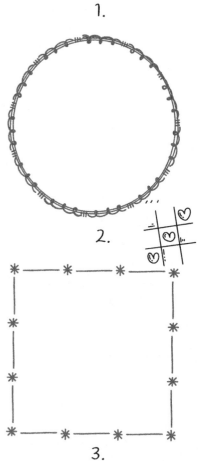

3.

3.

PAPER FORTUNE TELLER

LET'S LEARN ABOUT EACH OTHER WHILE PLAYING

TOGETHER

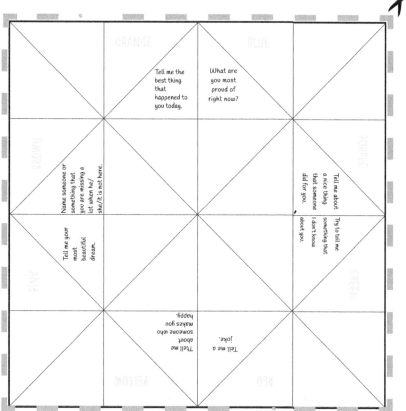

ORANGE — Tell me the best thing that happened to you today.

BLUE — What are you most proud of right now?

BROWN — Name someone or something that you are missing a lot when he/she/it is not here.

PINK — Tell me your most beautiful dream.

PURPLE — Tell me about a nice thing that someone did for you.

GREEN — Try to tell me something that I don't know about you.

YELLOW — Tell me about someone who makes you happy.

RED — Tell me a joke.

Instructions :

1. Cut the big square below by following the grey border.

2. Color the cases in which a color is written (with the right color).

3. Follow the folding instructions:

1. Take the square

2. Fold one corner...

3. ...Then the others to get to that shape

4. Flip the piece of paper

5. Fold one corner...

6. ...Then the others to get to that shape

7. Put your fingers underneath: your fortune teller is ready !

<u>Reminder</u>: To play, player 1 will put each thumb in a hole of the paper folding and place their index and their middle finger in the opposite hole. Player 2 will pick a number from 1 to 10. Player 1 will open and close their fingers as many times as the number chosen by player 2, who then picks a color that will match a question they will have to answer.

27

LET'S DANCE !

TOGETHER

LET'S HAVE FUN IN MUSIC...

Son, what is your favorite song ?

How does it make you feel ?

_____

_____

_____

Mom, what is your favorite song ?

How does it make you feel ?

_____

_____

Mission :

Let's listen to both songs and have fun
dancing together!

29

OUR EMOTIONS

SON, HOW ARE YOU FEELING RIGHT NOW ?

What makes you happy :

_____

_____

What makes you worried :

_____

_____

What makes you angry :

_____

_____

What makes you sad :

_____

_____

Would you need me to do anything to help?

_____

_____

OUR EMOTIONS

MOM, HOW ARE YOU FEELING RIGHT NOW ?

What makes you happy :

_____

_____

What makes you worried :

_____

_____

What makes you angry :

_____

_____

What makes you sad :

_____

_____

What do you think about what I wrote?

_____

_____

THE iDEAL JOB

SON

WHEN I GROW UP, I WILL BE...

What job would you like to have in the future?

What do you need to do to achieve that?

Draw or paste images to depict yourself in the future doing this job.

32

THE iDEAL JOB

MOM

WHEN I WAS LiTTLE, I WANTED TO BE...

What job did you want to have when you were a kid?

How is your life different today?

Draw or paste images that depict how you feel about your current work.

ELECTED BEST MOM

Mom, you always have time for ...

_____

_____

_____

You always make me feel special when ...

_____

_____

_____

Paste a photo of us filled with love!

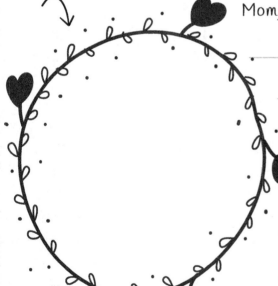

Mom, I love you because ....

_____

_____

_____

_____

CERTIFICATE OF A GOLDEN SON

Son, I'm proud to be your mom because ...

_____

_____

_____

I love that you ...

_____

_____

_____

Paste a photo of us filled with love!

Son, I love you because:

CHILDHOOD MEMORIES

 LET'S TALK ABOUT CHILDHOOD

Son, what do you think my childhood was like?
In your opinion, what do you think was different for me?

Do you think that my childhood was easier or harder than yours and why?

What is your favorite memory so far?

(Write or draw)

CHILDHOOD MEMORIES

LET'S TALK ABOUT CHILDHOOD

Mom, what was different during your childhood?

☆ _____   ☆ _____

☆ _____   ☆ _____

☆ _____   ☆ _____

What did you find better before?   ... And better now?

☆ _____   ☆ _____

☆ _____   ☆ _____

☆ _____   ☆ _____

☆ _____   ☆ _____

What is your best childhood memory?

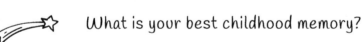
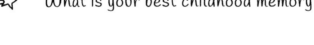

_____

_____

_____

_____

_____

_____

HELLO SADNESS

TOGETHER

HOW DO WE MANAGE iT?

Son, what do you do when you are sad?

_____

_____

_____

What helps you feel better?

_____

_____

_____

Next time you are sad, we could:

☐ Hug each other   ☐ Give each other kisses

☐ Share an activity   ☐ Stay in our little corners

☐ Discuss   ☐ _____

What about you? What helps you feel better when you are sad?

_____

_____

_____

<u>Mission</u>: We both invent a reusable formula to cheer up next time we are sad:

_____

SPACE COMPETITION

LET'S BUILD OUR VESSELS!

Let's build our own paper planes, decorate them and train to make them fly like professionals!

Rules: We will define a line dedicated to the launch and 3 other possible lines to reach giving you points: the first one will give 10 points, the second, a bit further will give 30 points, then the last one, the furthest, will give 50 points. The first person to get to 150 points will win (you can reduce to 100 points if needed)!

Instructions:

1) Fold the piece of paper in 2, then unfold.

2) Fold both top corners towards the center of the piece of paper to obtain this shape.

3) Fold to bring the exterior borders of the triangle on the middle line to obtain this shape.

 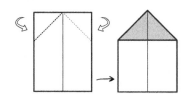 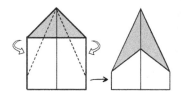

4) Fold completely in two to obtain this shape.

5) Fold a part of the wing by bringing the top point towards the bottom point, Same for the other wing.

6) Put the sides back up so they are horizontal when the plane is flying. The plane is ready, bravo!

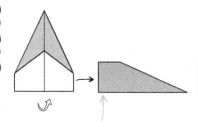 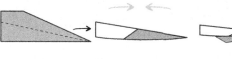

TOGETHER

FRIENDSHIP IS PRECIOUS...

Mom, who are your best friends?   What about you Son ?

♥ _____   ♥ _____

♥ _____   ♥ _____

♥ _____   ♥ _____

♥   ♥

For you Son, what does it mean to be a good friend?

_____

_____

_____

What about you Mom ? Describe the ideal friend.

_____

_____

_____

Son, write down the
nicest thing a friend has
ever told you:

TRAVEL TO THE FUTURE

IMAGINE HOW IT WOUD BE IF ...

How do you picture life on Earth in 200 years? What will be different?

_____

_____

_____

_____

What cool invention might be invented?
(You can even talk about something that is impossible nowadays)

_____

_____

Draw it!

TRAVEL TO THE FUTURE

IMAGINE HOW IT WOUD BE IF ...

MOM

How do you picture life on Earth in 200 years? What will be different?

_____

_____

_____

What cool invention might be invented?
(You can even talk about something that is impossible nowadays)

_____

_____

Draw it!

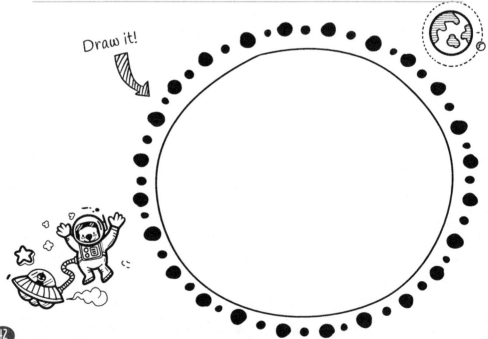

DO YOU LIKE IT OR NOT?

MOM

MOM, YOUR TURN TO GUESS IF I LIKE THESE THINGS OR NOT...

Tick the boxes and I will then correct it by circling the right answers!

	MY SON LOVES	SO SO	HE HATES
Walking in the sand	☐	☐	☐
Taking the train	☐	☐	☐
Mind games	☐	☐	☐
Spinach	☐	☐	☐
Taking a bath	☐	☐	☐
Strawberry ice-cream	☐	☐	☐
Costumes	☐	☐	☐
Chewing gum	☐	☐	☐
Going to the cinema	☐	☐	☐
Romantic movies	☐	☐	☐
Water fights	☐	☐	☐
Spicy sauce	☐	☐	☐
Spiders	☐	☐	☐
Crowd	☐	☐	☐
History-Geography	☐	☐	☐
Getting up early	☐	☐	☐
Ghosts stories	☐	☐	☐

I count how many right answers...

MOM, YOU HAVE   RIGHT ANSWERS!

43

DO YOU LiKE iT OR NOT?

SON

SON, YOUR TURN TO GUESS iF i LiKE THESE THiNGS OR NOT...

Tick the boxes and I will then correct it by circling the right answers!

	MOM LOVES	SO SO	SHE HATES
Walking in the sand	☐	☐	☐
Taking the train	☐	☐	☐
Mind games	☐	☐	☐
Spinach	☐	☐	☐
Taking a bath	☐	☐	☐
Strawberry ice-cream	☐	☐	☐
Costumes	☐	☐	☐
Chewing gum	☐	☐	☐
Going to the cinema	☐	☐	☐
Romantic movies	☐	☐	☐
Water fights	☐	☐	☐
Spicy sauce	☐	☐	☐
Spiders	☐	☐	☐
Crowd	☐	☐	☐
History-Geography	☐	☐	☐
Getting up early	☐	☐	☐
Ghosts stories	☐	☐	☐

I count how many right answers...

SON, YOU HAVE ___ RIGHT ANSWERS!

OUR BEST MEMORIES

THE TWO OF US: OUR MOST BEAUTIFUL MEMORIES

SON

Son, what is the best memory you have with me?

_____

_____

_____

Draw or glue a photo of this moment!

3 other great
things that we
have done
together:

 _____

_____

_____

OUR BEST MEMORIES

Mom, what is the best memory you have with me?

_____

_____

_____

Draw or glue a photo of this moment!

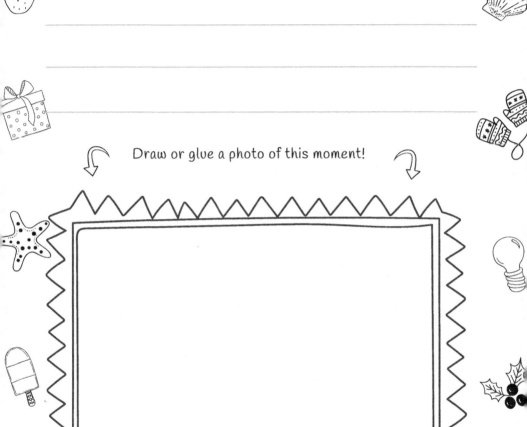

3 other great  _____
things that we
have done
together:

46

OUR CHARACTERS

QUALITIES AND FLAWS...

Son, what are your two main qualities?

What about your two biggest flaws?

What about you Mom, what are your two main qualities?

What about your two biggest flaws?

In the qualities and flaws list below, let's circle either in red or in blue the ones that define us the most. Let's agree before circling the answers!

Mom will circle in red.   The son will circle in blue.

courageous   organized   creative

                         dreamer   generous
anxious

     impulsive   sociable
                                          patient

  shy
              dynamic
                              stubborn

WHAT CONNECTS US

TOGETHER

OUR COMMON FEATURES AND OUR DIFFERENCES...

Son, write 2 things that we have in common:

♥ _____

♥ _____

Write 2 things that are different about us:

♥ _____

♥ _____

Mom, write 2 things that we have in common:

♥ _____

♥ _____

Write 2 things that are different about us:

♥ _____

♥ _____

BUT MOST IMPORTANTLY....
WE LOVE EACH OTHER !

PHOTOSHOOT

TODAY, WE ARE IN THE SPOTLIGHTS!

<u>Dare</u>: We will put on different outfits, we will take photos, we will glue the photos onto this page and mostly... we will have fun together!

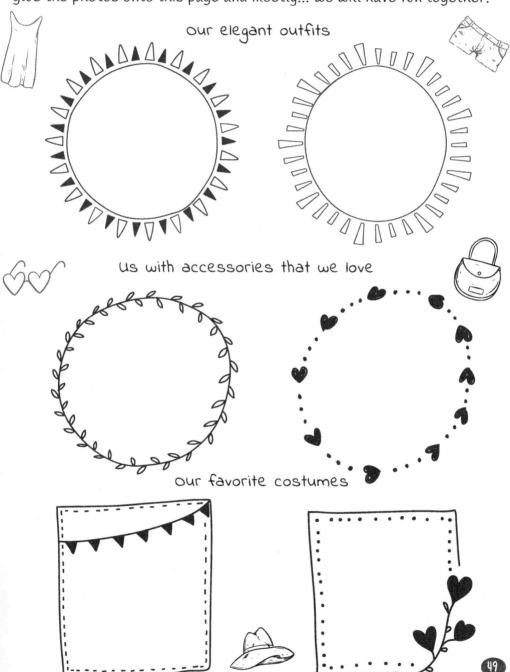

our elegant outfits

us with accessories that we love

our favorite costumes

49

BEING DIFFERENT

LET'S TALK ABOUT IT

Do you sometimes feel different from the others? Why?

_____

_____

_____

_____

Do you think it is good to be different?
How does it make you feel?

_____

_____

_____

_____

Would you like me to do something about it?

_____

_____

_____

_____

BEING DIFFERENT

LET'S TALK ABOUT IT

Mom, do you sometimes feel different from the others? Why?

_____

_____

_____

_____

Mom, what do you think of what I wrote about being different?
Do you think it is a good thing to be different?

_____

_____

_____

_____

_____

Maybe you can give me the name of a famous character (movie,
book...) or a celebrity who is really liked because of their
difference?

_____

_____

BETWEEN YOU AND ME...

Son, what was the most embarrassing moment that you have ever experienced?

_____

_____

_____

Tell me about a time when you were particularly proud of yourself.

_____

_____

_____

Mom, what was the most embarrassing moment that you have ever experienced?

_____

_____

_____

Tell me about a time when you were particularly proud of yourself.

_____

_____

_____

HAPPY BIRTHDAY!
THE CELEBRATION OF THIS SPECIAL DAY

SON

 What is the most beautiful gift you have ever received?

_____

_____

_____

What is your best birthday memory?

_____

_____

_____

Is there something in particular that you would like to do for your next birthday?

(Draw, write, glue what you would like to answer)

53

HAPPY BIRTHDAY!

THE CELEBRATION OF THIS SPECIAL DAY

MOM

What is the most beautiful gift you have ever received?

_____

_____

_____

What is your best birthday memory?

_____

_____

Is there something in particular that you would like to do for your next birthday?

(Draw, write, glue what you would like to answer)

RAINY DAY...

... HAPPY DAY?

TOGETHER

What we like to do the most on a rainy day:

	Mom	Son
⭐ Watch movies at home	☐	☐
⭐ Read a book	☐	☐
⭐ Play board games	☐	☐
⭐ Play video games	☐	☐
⭐ Draw	☐	☐
⭐ Puzzles	☐	☐
⭐ Cook desserts together	☐	☐
⭐ Go to the museum	☐	☐
⭐ Go shopping	☐	☐
⭐ Do a craft activity together	☐	☐
⭐ Go to the movies	☐	☐
⭐ Sleep in	☐	☐
⭐ _____	☐	☐
⭐ _____	☐	☐

What could we plan to do together next time it rains?

_____

_____

TOGETHER

SOMETIMES IT MAKES ME LAUGH, SOMETIMES IT ANNOYS ME...

Son, what do I say often in your opinion?

Mom, what do I say often in your opinion?

LOVE COLORING

SON

Mission: Cut this coloring, complete it with nice colors, and offer it to your mom!
Maybe hang it to remind yourself of how much you love each other! ;-)

LOVE COLORING

HONEY

I LOVE YOU endlessly

LET'S iMAGiNE THAT A TiME TRAVEL MACHiNE HAS BEEN iNVENTED...

You have a chance to go back in time and change something that has happened in your life: what would it be?

_____

_____

_____

If you could go back to any time in History, when would it be? What would you want to see? What would you do there?

_____

_____

_____

_____

▼ You can carry on describing what you will see, or you can draw it here: ▼

TRIP DOWN MEMORY LANE

MOM

LET'S IMAGINE THAT A TIME TRAVEL MACHINE HAS BEEN INVENTED...

You have a chance to go back in time and change something that has happened in your life: what would it be?

_____

_____

_____

If you could go back to any time in History, when would it be? What would you want to see? What would you do there?

_____

_____

_____

_____

You can carry on describing what you will see, or you can draw it here:

GRATITUDE, OUR ALLY

TODAY WILL BE A BEAUTIFUL DAY...

SON

Write why it is amazing to be alive:

_____

_____

_____

You are happy and grateful that these people love you:

_____

_____

Write down the activities that you feel lucky to be able to do:

_____

_____

_____

Draw or glue pictures of the best things in your life!

GRATITUDE, OUR ALLY

TODAY WILL BE A BEAUTIFUL DAY...

MOM

Write why it is amazing to be alive:

_____

_____

_____

You are happy and grateful that these people love you:

_____

_____

Write down the activities that you feel lucky to be able to do:

_____

_____

_____

Draw or glue pictures of the best things in your life!

BOOKS AND US

AN IMAGINARY WORLD...

Son, what is your favorite book ?

_____

_____

If you had to write a book about your life, what would the title be?

_____

Mom, what was your favorite book as a child? And now?

_____

_____

If you had to write a book about your life, what would the title be?

_____

Let's draw the portrait of our favorite book character!

Mom   Son

LET'S DRAW TOGETHER

TOGETHER

WE CREATE IMAGINARY ANIMALS... LET'S GO!

PS: let's draw as many details as possible

Together, let's draw a "zebrox" (half zebra, half fox)!

Let's draw a "chickonkey" (half chick, half monkey)!

ROCK-PAPER-SCISSORS

 LET'S PLAY!

TOGETHER

The game can be played in two different sessions (10 games each).
The player with most points will win at the end!

Reminder: Both players will get their hands out at the same time from
behind their back and show a rock, paper or scissors with their hands.
Rock beats scissors, scissors beat paper and paper beats rock.

PART 1

GAME	MOM	SON
1		
2		
3		
4		
5		
6		
7		
8		
9		
10		
TOTAL		

PART 2

GAME	MOM	SON
1		
2		
3		
4		
5		
6		
7		
8		
9		
10		
TOTAL		

BECAUSE WE ARE UNIQUE...

... AND IMPORTANT! LET'S CELEBRATE OUR ASSETS

SON

What do you think you are best at? What are your strengths?

Are you comfortable with your body?

What are your favorite parts of your body?

♥

♥

♥

You know very well how to do that alone:

68

BECAUSE WE ARE UNIQUE...

... AND IMPORTANT! LET'S CELEBRATE OUR ASSETS

MOM

Mom, what do you think about what I wrote? Do you agree? What do you consider as my biggest strengths?

_____

_____

_____

_____

_____

_____

_____

_____

_____

What about you, Mom? What are you best at?

☆ _____

☆ _____

☆ _____

☆ _____

WiNTER...

AND EVERYTHING THAT GOES WITH IT!

Do you like this season and are you looking forward to it? Why?

_____

_____

_____

_____

Tell me what makes you think about winter
and what you like the most about this season:

☆ _____   ☆ _____

☆ _____   ☆ _____

☆ _____   ☆ _____

☆ _____   ☆ _____

☆ _____   ☆ _____

☆ _____   ☆ _____

Give me a song title that you associate with winter:

WINTER...

AND EVERYTHING THAT GOES WITH IT!

Do you like this season and are you looking forward to it? Why?

_____

_____

_____

_____

Tell me what makes you think about winter
and what you like the most about this season:

☆ _____   ☆ _____

☆ _____   ☆ _____

☆ _____   ☆ _____

☆ _____   ☆ _____

☆ _____   ☆ _____

☆ _____   ☆ _____

Give me a song title that you associate with winter:

A PERFECT DAY

A LITTLE BIT OF IMAGINATION

SON

Imagine your ideal day.
Where would you go? What would you do? With whom?

Draw/ glue what inspires you.

A PERFECT DAY

A LiTTLE BiT OF iMAGiNATiON

Imagine your ideal day.
Where would you go? What would you do? With whom?

Draw/ glue what inspires you.

LET'S LIST OUR FANCIES

EVERYTHING WE WOULD LIKE TO DO TOGETHER

How about filling in a table of goal/activities that we would like to do together?
We can get ideas from that list to fill in on the next page!

-Sleep under the stars

-Take a hot air balloon ride

-Go snorkeling

-Do yoga together

-Go horse riding on the beach

-Visit a volcano

-Have a bath in hot springs

-Volunteer for a charity

-Go zip lining in the forest

-Play an escape game together

-Go into a haunted house

-Sing karaoke as a duo

-Grow aromatic plants

-Go wales watching in nature

-Watch fireworks from the beach

-Say "yes" to everything for a day (with limits)

-Do a big puzzle together

-Try every dish in our favorite restaurant

-Visit an animal refuge

-Go wild camping

-Go to a trampoline park

-Watch sun set together

-Take photos in a themed PhotoBox

-Watch shooting stars

-Create our family tree

-Go on a tandem ride

-Get lost into a maze in a cornfield

-Go on a treasure hunt together

-Create a time capsule together (with our memories) and open it in 10 years

-Spend a night in an unusual accommodation

-Have a water fight

-Treat ourselves to a spa day

-Go and see a musical

-Exchange 100% homemade Christmas gifts

-Go on a Safari (eco-responsible) in a Jeep

-Go on a sled dog ride

-Have a movie marathon

-Go Kayaking together

-Go to a festival together

-Go up the Empire State Building in N'

-Watch a cocoon become a butterfly

-Create a pottery together

-Go skating together

-Play laser game or paintball together (if minimum age required)

-Make sandcastles

-Try a new theme park

-Fly a kite

-Go ice skating during the holidays

OUR (SMALL & BIG) DREAMS TOGETHER

TOGETHER

(Let's pencil a date on which we would like to have accomplished one goal: tick the box "done" and put the date of accomplishment when the goal is reached!)

N°	GOAL	DATE	DONE

WE HAVE SUPER POWERS

AND WE DREAM A LITTLE!

SON

Rank these powers in the order you would like to have them:

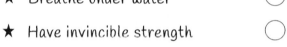

★ Read people's minds ◯

★ Fly into the air ◯

★ Control time ◯

★ Breathe under water ◯

★ Have invincible strength ◯

Why did you pick this order?

_____

_____

What would you do if you could be invisible?

_____

_____

What would you do if you could read people's minds?

_____

_____

... and if you had invincible strength?

_____

_____

WE HAVE SUPER POWERS

AND WE DREAM A LITTLE!

MOM

Rank these powers in the order you would like to have them:

★ Read people's minds ◯

★ Fly into the air ◯

★ Control time ◯

★ Beathe under water ◯

★ Have invincible strength ◯

Why did you pick this order?

_____

_____

What would you do if you could be invisible?

_____

_____

What would you do if you could read people's minds?

_____

_____

... and if you had invincible strength?

_____

_____

OUR SUCCESS STORIES

SON

OUR OWN VICTORIES!

Son, what are your biggest achievements according to you?

_____

_____

_____

What is the most courageous thing that you have ever done?

_____

_____

What is the most courageous thing that I have ever done (according to you) ?

_____

_____

Think about how you felt when you achieved those things and draw yourself that way.

OUR SUCCESS STORIES

OUR OWN VICTORIES!

Mom, what do you think about what I wrote?

_____

_____

_____

_____

_____

_____

_____

What are your biggest achievements?

_____

_____

_____

_____

FUNNY FACES COMPETITION

TOGETHER

WE TAKE PHOTOS OF US WHILE PULLING FUNNY FACES...

.... and we will remember them by putting the best ones in the journal!

OUR VALUES

THAT GUIDE OUR LIVES

TOGETHER

We will each select the 10 values that are the most important to us and we will explain why.

Mom will circle her values.   The son will color his values.

LOVE

BENEVOLENCE

RESPECT

SINCERITY

FAITH

FRIENDSHIP

KINDNESS

COURAGE

TOLERANCE

CREATIVITY

MUTUAL HELP

TRUST

FREEDOM

PERSEVERANCE

JUSTICE

SHARING

INDEPENDENCE

WORK

RESPONSIBILITY

FAMILY

Are there any other values that we would like to add?

_____

_____

VACATION TIME!

IS IT SOON ... ?

We can't wait to go on vacation to:

SON: _____

MOM: _____

What is our favorite memory of holidays together?

_____

_____

_____

_____

We draw or paste a photo os this memory :

WHAT DO YOU PREFER?

TOGETHER

LET'S COMPARE OUR PREFERENCES AND LAUGH A BIT!

(From the simplest question... to the most unusual and funny!)

SON	MOM				SON	MOM
☐	☐	strawberry	OR	chocolate	☐	☐
☐	☐	city	OR	countryside	☐	☐
☐	☐	morning	OR	evening	☐	☐
☐	☐	scuba diving	OR	skiing	☐	☐
☐	☐	controlling fire	OR	water	☐	☐
☐	☐	living in a theme park	OR	in a zoo	☐	☐
☐	☐	sleeping in a tent	OR	in a hotel	☐	☐

Let's make it a bit more complicated...

SON	MOM				SON	MOM
☐	☐	having 2m long arms	OR	50cm long legs	☐	☐
☐	☐	having bunny ears	OR	a pig's tail	☐	☐
☐	☐	never going to the toilet again	OR	never having to sleep again	☐	☐
☐	☐	having the power to become an owl	OR	a dolphin	☐	☐
☐	☐	being super fast	OR	able to freeze time	☐	☐
☐	☐	having grass as hair	OR	a carrot as a nose	☐	☐
☐	☐	being hairy as a bear	OR	having scales all over your body	☐	☐
☐	☐	cuddling a spider	OR	kissing a snake	☐	☐
☐	☐	being able to read people's mind	OR	to see the future	☐	☐
☐	☐	never reading books again	OR	never watching movies again	☐	☐

CATEGORIES GAME

LET'S PLAY!

Instructions : Copy this table on two pieces of paper so you both have one.
Taking turns, players will pick a letter of the alphabet and work alone
find names associated with each category as fast as possible.

Letter	Fruit or Veggie	Country/City	Job	Animal	Boy name	Girl name	Brand	Musical instrument	Score

Total score

AROUND THE WORLD

SAFE TRAVELS

SON

If you could go anywhere on Earth, where would you go?

_____

The farthest you have been is: _____

How many countries have you visited? _____

Which one did you like the most, and why?

_____

_____

Put a tick next to where you have been and put a heart next to where you would like to go:

(You can use a detailed map if necessary)

AROUND THE WORLD

SAFE TRAVELS

MOM

If you could go anywhere on Earth, where would you go?

_____

The farthest you have been is: _____

How many countries have you visited? _____

Which one did you like the most, and why?

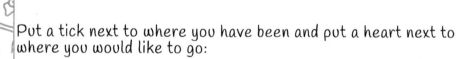

_____

_____

Put a tick next to where you have been and put a heart next to where you would like to go:

EXQUISITE CORPSE

 LET'S PLAY WITH **WORDS!**

<u>Instructions</u>: Cut the game sheet below (or use another way to copy this model) and fold it like an accordion following the lines.

Taking turns, each player will write a part of a sentence and fold it to hide what they wrote. When the sentence is completed, we can laugh while discovering the story!

subject

verb

complement

subject

verb

complement

subject

verb

complement

CHILDHOOD MEMORIES

MOM, I ALSO WANT TO KNOW...

What were your like as a kid?

_____

_____

_____

_____

What was your favorite game? _____

What was your favorite age? _____

How was Grandma back then ?

_____

_____

_____

_____

What about your house ?

_____

_____

_____

THINGS WE DON'T LIKE

TOGETHER

EVERYTHING THAT DISGUSTS US AND MAKES US SCARED...

 Son, tell me one thing that you find disgusting:

_____

 What are you most scared about?

_____

Is there something that you will never try/do ?

_____

Mom, tell me one thing that you find disgusting:

_____

 What are you most scared about?

_____

Is there something that you will never try/do ?

_____

Is there something that were are scared about but that
we would face if we were together?

_____

OUR DREAMS & GOALS

>>> LET'S DREAM A BIT... ⭐

Can you give me 3 goals/dreams that you have?

☆ _____

☆ _____

☆ _____

How could you achieve them ?

_____

_____

_____

_____

Draw yourself making your dreams come true.

OUR DREAMS & GOALS

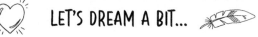

LET'S DREAM A BIT...   MOM

Mom, what do you think about what I wrote ?

_____

_____

_____

_____

_____

Are there any dreams you still want to fulfill?

(Write, draw, paste a picture...)

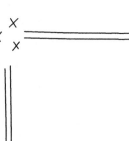

LET'S LAUGH TOGETHER

... IT'S VERY HEALTHY !

Who is the funniest person we know?

Mom: ☆ _____

Son: ☆ _____

Let's quote something that makes us laugh a lot:

Mom: ☆ _____

Son: ☆ _____

Son, tell me your funniest memory:

_____

_____

_____

What about you mom, what is yours?

_____

_____

_____

<u>Mission</u>: Let's make each other laugh; tell a joke, pull funny faces, tickle each other... everything is allowed!

93

JOY + KiNDNESS...

... = A MORE BEAUTiFUL WORLD !

When was the last time you did something nice for someone?
What was it?

_____

_____

_____

Why did you do it and how did it make you feel?

_____

_____

_____

Have you ever experienced joy for your me, your mom, or for
someone else? When was it?

_____

_____

_____

_____

JOY + KiNDNESS...

... = A MORE BEAUTIFUL WORLD !

When was the last time you did something nice for someone?
What was it?

_____

_____

_____

Why did you do it and how did it make you feel?

_____

_____

_____

Have you ever experienced joy for me, your son? When was it?

_____

_____

_____

_____

_____

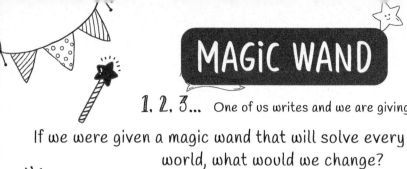

MAGIC WAND

TOGETHER

1, 2, 3... One of us writes and we are giving ideas together!

If we were given a magic wand that will solve every problem in the world, what would we change?

_____

_____

_____

_____

_____

_____

_____

We draw/ paste pictures/ write about our ideal world

NAVAL BATTLE

TOGETHER

HiT... SUNK!

Player 1

	1	2	3	4	5	6	7	8	9	10
A										
B										
C										
D										
E										
F										
G										
H										
i										
J										

1 aircraft carrier

5 squares

1 cruiser

4 squares

2 submarines

3 squares + 3 squares

1 torpedo boat

2 squares

◯ in the water

X hit

Rules :

Facing each other, each player will place their boats on the grid, vertically or horizontally, by coloring the corresponding squares in grey. Both will hide their piece of paper, then taking turns, they will tell the other where they are hitting by giving a number and a letter (ex: c2). When a boat is hit, we will put a cross and a circle when it is in the water. When a player sinks a boat, they will play again. Finally, one of the players will win when he has sunk all the other player's boats.

Player 2

	1	2	3	4	5	6	7	8	9	10
A										
B										
C										
D										
E										
F										
G										
H										
i										
J										

LET'S AIM FOR THE MOON

... IN THE WORST CASE, WE WILL REACH THE STARS

TOGETHER

Son, what would you do if you were sure you would not fail?

What is your favorite saying?

You feel strong when....

Mom, what would you do if you were sure you would not fail?

What is your favorite saying ?

You feel strong when....

AT SCHOOL

EVERYTHING WE LOVE (AND THE REST)

What are your favorite subjects?

And the ones you like the least?

In general what do you like at school?

And what do you dislike? Is there anything that stresses you?

AT SCHOOL

EVERYTHING WE LOVE (AND THE REST)

What were your favorite subjects?

And the ones you liked the least?

In general what did you like at school?

And what did you dislike?

GOOD NIGHT...

... AND SWEET DREAMS!

Son, what you prefer at bedtime is:

Before sleeping, you often think about:

Mom, what you prefer at bedtime is:

Before sleeping, you often think about:

<u>Mission</u>: We make up a sign to say good night!

OUR FAMILY

AND WHAT WE LIKE TO DO TOGETHER

SON

Son, what is your favorite thing to do with me?

What have you always liked doing with Grandma?
And what do you particulary like about her?

What do you like to do with the rest of the family?

☆ What is your favorite family tradition? ☆

OUR FAMILY

AND WHAT WE LIKE TO DO TOGETHER

Mom, what is your favorite thing to do with me?

_____

What have you always liked doing with your mom?
And what do you particulary admire about her?

_____

_____

_____

What do you like to do with the rest of the family?

_____

_____

_____

_____

☆   What is your favorite family tradition?   ☆

_____

HELLO ANGER

HOW DO WE MANAGE iT?

Son, what do you do when you are angry?

_____

_____

_____

What helps you calm down ?

_____

_____

_____

Mom, what do you think about what I wrote? Do you have any suggestions? What do you do to calm yourself down when you are angry?

_____

_____

_____

_____

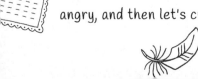

<u>Mission</u>: Together, let's write on a piece of paper what makes us angry, and then let's crumple it and tear it apart into small pieces!

IN 20 YEARS...

LET'S THINK ABOUT OUR FUTURE?

Son, how do you see your life in 20 years?
Where would you be ? What would you do? With whom?

What about you Mom? How do you imagine your life?

TOGETHER

THE END...

BUT THE BEGINNING OF OTHER ADVENTURES!

Mom, is there any advice you would like to give me today?

_____

_____

_____

_____

⭐ THAT'S IT, WE'VE FINISHED COMPLETING THE JOURNAL! ⭐

What did we like about writing in this journal?

Son:

_____

_____

Mom:

_____

_____

☆ What can we do to celebrate our journal's completion ? ☆

(a special activity?)

_____

We will read our journal again on that date : _____

♥ NOTES BETWEEN US ♥

Printed in Great Britain
by Amazon